Old Armadale and Blackrid[

John Hood

A surprising number of the properties seen here in this early view of West Main Street, just east of Academy Street, have survived. These include Pianotown House, the two-storey whitewashed building on the left. This was once the home of Dr William Anderson, a well-loved local doctor who reputedly was the owner of one of the first motor cars to grace the roads in and around Armadale. A few doors along from Pianotown House is a cottage with two dormer windows, which at one time was occupied by Peter Borza's ice cream café. Peter, or, more properly, Pasquale, took over the café from a Mr Forte and continued in business until around 1950. He was particularly renowned for his twopenny plates of vinegar-drenched boiled peas, which he would sell during the winter months when demand for ice cream was low. In 1969 the café was taken over by Nicandro and Concetta Coia who, in addition to making their own ice cream, sold coffees, teas and milkshakes. Today the business is run by James and Giorgio Coia, Nicandro and Concetta's sons.

Indisputably, Armadale's best-known building must be the Goth public house on West Main Street, designed by architect Thomas Roberts. With its distinctive leaning clock tower, complete with louvred octagonal cap, its establishment as the Armadale Public House Society in 1901 came amid local concern for the alleged excessive drinking by Armadale's drouthy citizens – a move strongly supported by individuals such as Baillie (later Provost) Robert Smith. The Goth was modelled on an experiment first carried out in Gothenburg, Sweden, whereby council-controlled licensed premises (which also provided coffee and hot meals) were set up in such a way as to allow a portion of the profits to be set aside for community projects. In 1924, to mark 21 years of service by its first President, Malcolm Mallace (often referred to as 'Auld Malkum'), the architects Peddie & Kinnear were commissioned to design an art nouveau columned interior and clock tower. The clock tower was refurbished in 1995.

© 2007 John Hood
First Published in the United Kingdom, 2008
Stenlake Publishing Limited
54–58 Mill Square, Catrine, KA5 6RD
www.stenlake.co.uk
ISBN 9781840334166

Further Reading

The books listed below were used by the author during his research. None are available from Stenlake Publishing; please contact your local bookshop or reference library.

J. Borrowman, *Blackridge Yesteryear: A Local History* (n.d.).

S. Borrowman, *Behind God's Back: The Story of Blackridge*, Bathgate: Blackridge Community Council (2005).

W. F. Hendrie, *Armadale in Old Picture Postcards*, Zaltbommel: European Library (1998).

History of Armadale Association, *Tales Fae the 'Dale* (1989).

History of Armadale Association, *Mair Tales Fae the 'Dale* (1990).

History of Armadale Association, *Picturing the Past: A Photographic Look at Old Armadale*, 3 vols, Edinburgh: Print Consultancy (1998–2005).

INTRODUCTION

Before the opening, in the 1790s, of a new turnpike road (or 'Great Road') linking Edinburgh and Glasgow, Blackridge and Armadale were little more than small agricultural communities. Indeed, the former, situated about two miles west of Armadale, was at that time no more than a series of separate 'fermtouns' (homesteads of farms) clustered around Bedlormie, Blackridge and Wester Craigs, and all within the ancient Barony of Ogilface. Being roughly equidistant from Edinburgh and Glasgow, Blackridge was a convenient change stop for the several stagecoaches using this new road on a daily basis. In 1862 the railway network first came to the area, to allow for the transport of quarried coal and whinstone. Later, around 1871, a regular passenger service was also provided for Blackridge residents. However, the 1871 census revealed that there were hardly more than 100 persons living in Blackridge. About a decade later this situation changed dramatically, when pits were sunk in the vicinity of the village at Blackrigg, Northrigg and Westrigg. This industry, together with the associated quarrying activities, transformed Blackridge – so much so that the 1901 census shows the population as numbering approximately 797, and that of Westrigg (which was then considered to be a separate community) approximately 488. The village's new-found prosperity resulted in an improvement in local educational facilities, the erection of churches and a public hall, and the increasing variety of local shops that were established. This prosperity was, however, almost wholly dependent on the strength of its mining industry, and the eventual closure of the local collieries as the coal seams became exhausted spelled the end of the boom years. The population peaked around the 2,000 mark in 1951, but it is no coincidence that, after the closure of the last local colliery in 1955, the population of Blackridge began a slow and steady decline. Today, the village has a population of around 1,600 and most of those who are in employment now have to commute to neighbouring towns.

A not dissimilar situation applies to Armadale, or 'the Dale' as it is generally referred to locally. Even more than Blackridge, Armadale benefited from its strategic position on the Great Road, as it had the added advantage of being at a crossroads of a second major road running from north to south. Not surprisingly, the first settlement here, at Barbauchlaw as it was then known, developed around this crossroads. The present name of Armadale came from Sir William Honeyman, an advocate who purchased the estate of Barbauchlaw in 1790: on his elevation to the bench in 1797 he took the title of Lord Armadale (from his mother's estate in Sutherland) and this name was then applied to the township. As in Blackridge, the discovery of large coal deposits, and also ironstone, in the mid-1800s attracted the attention of several major coal and iron companies. They bought the mineral rights from local landlords, such as the Baillies of Polkemmet, and proceeded to sink pits all over the area. This in turn attracted several railway companies into the area. The influx of workers, both to work the mines and build the railways, led to the need for more housing, schooling for their children, and places of worship. Notwithstanding the richness of its mineral wealth, by the late 1800s, when the Glasgow coal master James Wood turned his attention to Armadale, many of the older pits had closed down and the town was suffering a downturn in its fortunes. Almost single-handedly Wood set about reopening pits and developing the associated brickmaking and steel industries. His endeavours revitalised the area and gradually other industries were introduced. However, like Blackridge, Armadale was largely dependent on its mineral deposits for its prosperity, and as the seams became exhausted and the pits closed, many of the miners moved away. The opening of the Polkemmet pit in 1922 stemmed the exodus to some extent. Later, when the British Motor Corporation truck and tractor plant at nearby Bathgate was opened in 1960, there was a further boost to the town's fortunes. Today, although there is some local industry, many residents have to travel beyond Armadale to their place of employment.

Acknowledgements

I would like to thank the following people for their help during my research: James Coia, Christine and Sandy Duncan, Betty Hunter, Linda Loch, Norman and Tom Sinnet, and Clark Steele. In particular, I would like to thank Sybil Cavanagh, Local History Librarian, West Lothian Libraries, for her generous assistance during my research, and Stuart Borrowman, Ron Dingwall and Betty Hunter, for commenting on the completed manuscript. The publishers gratefully acknowledge West Lothian Local History Library for the picture on the page opposite and pictures on pages 5, 13, 34, 38, 41 and on the back cover.

One of the highlights of the annual Armadale Children's Gala Day was the parade along East and West Main Streets. As the sender of this postcard makes clear, on this occasion the weather was, unfortunately, less than kind – not that it appears to have curtailed the attendance. This annual celebration was first held on Saturday, 9 June 1900, to mark the recent capture of Pretoria during the Boer War. In that year (which, incidentally, was also wet – and windy) the parade, headed by the Armadale Brass and Armadale Diamond Jubilee Bands, made its way through the town towards the Volunteer Field, where refreshments were provided. In 1902 the venue for the Gala Day refreshments was switched to the newly opened James Wood Public Park. The park, named in honour of one of Armadale's most generous benefactors, was officially opened on 26 June 1902.

Within a few years of its inception, no Children's Gala Day was considered complete without flags and bunting, decorated horse-drawn floats and floral arches. The floral arches in particular were very impressive indeed. Designed and constructed by the miners and their families, these massive structures of single, double or even triple arches were traditionally located at various points throughout the town. They proved a popular attraction, as witnessed by the crowd seen here in 1907 beside the floral arches at Davy Young's grocery shop in South Street. Work on these arches would usually continue well into the evening preceding Gala Day, and it is said that on these occasions it would take a lot of persuasion to get local children to bed, because they wanted to stay up and watch all the activity – and no doubt they were already excited at the thought of the next day's festivities.

Before the establishment of the Bathgate Landward School Board in 1873, local children were taught either at the publicly funded Armadale Subscription School in South Street or at one of the several Works Schools established by the local mining companies. Although it was the Board's initial intention to build straight away a new and much larger school in Academy Street, a long-running dispute with the Subscription School Committee meant that work did not proceed until 1877. Finally, in 1878, the first of several school buildings comprising the new Armadale Public School was opened. Situated in Academy Street, the new school could accommodate 530 pupils. By 1911, and with a school roll exceeding 1,300, the handsome three-storey block seen here was opened. In this view, taken around 1925, a class appears to be lined up in front of the Senior School building outside the main hall, preparing to enter the school by the girls' entrance (on the left).

This Armadale Public School class photograph – regrettably undated, but probably taken in the early 1900s – shows some of the children outside one of the Academy Street buildings. Although the constant hardships (including lack of proper nourishment and good footwear) suffered by mining families are well documented, these children do appear to be reasonably well clad and well fed. However, a common thread running through the booklet *Mair Tales Fae the 'Dale* is people recalling how they had to go to school in their bare feet. They also remembered the stigma (at least in their minds) associated with being taken by their parents to the local Parish Offices (situated above Fraser's butcher's shop) to get money to buy 'pairish' boots. This poverty may account for a particular childhood chant, which goes:

> Teacher, teacher let me in,
> Ma feet's cauld, ma shin's din.
> If you dinnae let me in,
> We'll no' come back in the efternin.

Since 1900, when this photograph was taken, most of the properties seen here on the eastern side of South Street have disappeared. These include the corner property which contained Brown Brothers' licensed grocery and tea merchant's, and, alongside, Ezzi's café and fish restaurant. This business was founded by Vincenzo Ezzi and was continued in the 1930s by his son Alfred. Among the early businesses further up South Street were Robert Brown's barber's shop and, in the two-storey building beyond the row of single-storey cottages, a plumber's owned by David Marr. As well as owning the barber's shop, Robert Brown was the author of an early history of Armadale, and is said to have been a very 'dapper' fellow, whose trademark dress was felt hat and spats. In the 1930s some of the cottages on the left were demolished to make way for the Regal Cinema, which was opened in 1936. With the closure of the cinema in 1972, the site was redeveloped. Today West Lothian Council Information Services occupy the corner site.

Until October 1907, when a Chapel School was officially opened in South Street by Father McGettigan of Musselburgh, Armadale's Catholic worshippers had to travel to Bathgate, Blackburn or Whitburn to attend services. In effect the new building was dual-purpose, having seven classrooms (which could accommodate 360 pupils), while it could also be used for religious services, when the partitions that normally acted as classroom dividers were pulled back. However, in 1925 church services were transferred to an ex-Territorial Hall in High Academy Street, which was renamed The Sacred Heart, thus allowing the original Chapel School to be used solely for educational purposes. In May 1974 The Sacred Heart was replaced by a new purpose-built building known as The Sacred Heart of St Anthony's, which was officially opened by His Grace Archbishop Keith O'Brien of St Andrews. The Chapel School, likewise, was later replaced by the new St Anthony's Primary School, at which time secondary pupils transferred to St Kentigern's in Blackburn.

Among the older properties seen in this view of West Main Street, taken around 1907, are (on the far left) the Crown Hotel (at that time under the management of James B. Greig) and, directly opposite, Elizabeth Kerr's People's Drapery Warehouse. The hotel, occupying a prominent position at the corner of West Main Street and South Street, was opened in 1857. Shortly after this photograph was taken, it came under new management and advertised that it was now 'thoroughly equipped to suit commercial gentlemen and visitors' and could provide 'every home comfort'. The drapery, which was active between 1900 and 1910, occupied an equally prominent position at the corner of West Main Street and North Street. Other businesses on the south side of the street at this time were Nathaniel (Natali) Benassi's café, which adjoined the Crown Hotel, and, further along, Alex Graham's grocery shop, Alex Hutton's ironmongery and workshop, Alex Mathieson (shoemaker) and, at 23–25 West Main Street, Dr John Anderson's chemist's shop.

By the early twentieth century, probably the most significant presence on the north side of West Main Street was the Armadale Co-operative Society, whose suite of shops can be seen to the west of John and Mary Archer's newspaper shop. First established in 1861, the Armadale Co-operative Society ceased trading in 1866, but was resurrected in 1873 and, after almost a century of independence, merged in 1972 with the West Calder Co-operative Society. In 1982 the latter was taken over by the Scottish Midland Co-operative Society. Since the early 1950s, when this photograph was taken, all of the Co-operative buildings seen here, with the exception of the extreme right-hand portion nearest the camera, have been demolished and replaced with a new-build Scotmid store. The surviving portion (with the carved lintels above the four upper windows) previously housed the bakery and drapery departments, but today is occupied by a branch of R. S. McColl. To the east of Archer's shop, alongside the Standard 10 motor car, is the Regal Bar.

The new Co-operative store on West Main Street (part of whose frontage can be seen here) eventually became the largest store in Armadale. As such, it was a far cry from the modest ground-floor shop opened by Armadale's first Co-operative Society at the foot of Bullion Brae in the early 1860s. Initially the West Main Street store was confined within a property known as McDonald's Hall but, under the able management of their first Secretary, Alex Mallace, in 1879 an adjoining bakery was acquired. From 1886 onwards, other neighbouring properties were also acquired and the whole was rebuilt on several occasions. By about 1905, the 'big store' (as it became known) was a general store, housing the grocery, bread, furniture and crockery departments, in addition to a drapery and boot department, and a separate butcher shop – all housed at ground level. Above these were a boardroom, a library, a tailors' workshop and a dressmakers' workshop. In this picture, the staff of the various departments pose at the entrance to the pend which gave access to the stables and van-rooms at the rear of the building.

One of the longest-established businesses on West Main Street was Archer's newsagent's shop. Daniel and Agnes Archer began trading in the 1870s with one shop, but before long other shops were opened at St Helen's Place in South Street and at Bathville Cross, with yet another in nearby Whitburn. Because of the location of the three Armadale shops, they were often referred to by the family as the 'bottom', 'middle' and 'top' shops. Eventually, the business was run by Daniel and Agnes's son John, together with his sister Mary. In addition to running the family business, John was also something of a local impresario, who successfully organised concerts and was instrumental in attracting personalities of the calibre of Sir Harry Lauder to appear in his shows. By the late 1970s the last remaining shop in the business (the West Main Street one) was sold to R. S. McColl. They occupied the premises briefly, before moving next door to their present location.

In the early years of the last century, George and Elizabeth Farquhar set up in business in Armadale. Their main shop was the Bee-Hive Drapery Stores in South Street, which had previously been a drapery run by a David Finlay. In addition, the Farquhars had another shop around the corner in West Main Street. This second shop (which had also been a drapery, run by James Alexander Bryden) specialised in millinery and dressmaking. Although no photograph appears to exist of the West Main Street shop, this photo (showing, perhaps, George, his wife and their staff) of the South Street shop gives us some indication of the wide range of goods for sale – in addition to clothing, there would appear to be soft furnishings, toys, musical instruments and jewellery on display. By 1929 only the South Street shop was owned by the family, and that was in Mrs Farquhar's name alone. In 1933 the shop was taken over by Mrs Agnes Friel.

Since the mid-1950s, when this photograph was taken, new building has taken place on both sides of South Street, most notably on the left of the picture, on the site of the former East Church and hall. These buildings, together with Marr's newsagent's, were demolished in the early 1980s to make way for the new Ochilview Court sheltered housing complex. Today a modest plaque mounted on the front wall of 2 Ochilview Court is the only tangible reminder of the church. Another casualty of the redevelopment which has taken place since 1955 is the single-storey whitewashed cottage near the church hall, just left of the black Ford Prefect car. This was once the home of Sir Hugh Roberton, founder of the renowned Glasgow Orpheus Choir. One building that has survived is the two-storey whitewashed building further down on the west side of South Street, at the corner of George Street. This is at present the Highlander Hotel.

Before 1860 local worshippers had to travel to Bathgate to attend the Free Church there. In that year the renowned Scottish obstetrician, Sir James Young Simpson (who was also a member of Bathgate's Free Church), laid the foundation stone of the new Armadale Free Church. Situated 'at the head of the hill' in South Street, this new church was built almost opposite the new Armadale Subscription School. Later, after the church was finished, the congregation set about raising funds for a church hall, assisted by a supposedly anonymous donation of £200, which was widely thought to be the gift of Lady Gillespie of Torbanehill, granddaughter of Lord Armadale. The congregation purchased and converted two houses opposite the church, which they named the Christian Institute. The institute was later sold and replaced, around 1901, by the larger purpose-built church hall seen here to the north of the church. On the left can be seen Mrs A. Marr's long-established bookseller's and stationery shop. In the summer of 1908, the 389-strong congregation of the Armadale United Free Church, as it was by then, unanimously selected the Rev. W. G. Kirk as their new minister. Kirk (see inset) had been brought up and educated in Kirkcaldy, and was a graduate of both Edinburgh (where he qualified as a chemist) and Glasgow Universities. He studied at the Glasgow College of the United Free Church, and before taking up his charge at Armadale, had been assistant to ministers in Ayr and Glasgow. He served as minister of Armadale United Free Church until 1919. In 1931 the United Free Church was renamed the East Church, to distinguish it from the former Parish (now West) Church. It was demolished in 1976 when the East and West Churches amalgamated.

On 11 November 1895 a meeting was held to discuss the purchase, and conversion to a town hall and council chamber, of the former Armadale Subscription School in South Street. Despite there being some objection to this proposal (local landowner and businessman James Wood felt that the chosen site was 'unsafe to build a Public Hall … until the ground has settled after coal is worked out'), it was agreed to proceed with the project. The following year, local landowner George Readman of Barbauchlaw bought the Subscription School for £700 and presented it free of charge to the town. After conversion, the new town hall was officially opened by Readman on 4 December 1896, with a grand concert and ball. In 1911, having failed to obtain further funding from Readman for alterations to the hall, the town gratefully accepted a generous donation of £1,000 from James Wood. Among its many uses, the town hall provided an excellent venue for the local Armadale Silver Band practice sessions which, if this pre-First World War photograph is anything to go by, attracted a ready audience.

Before 1881 the four-mile stretch of road from Woodside Toll, near Torphichen, to Armadale Cross was known as Branch Street. Thereafter it was renamed North Street. At the Cross stood a single-storey toll house and bar, which had been erected on the north-east corner around 1795. Until 15 May 1855, when the Forbes-Mackenzie Act restricting the sale of alcohol was passed, 'old John' the toll keeper dispensed beer and spirits to passing trade. This was, in effect, Armadale's first licensed premises. Additionally, the toll house doubled as a dairy – locals, seeing customers wending their way home under the influence, used to remark that they 'had been for the milk again'! None of the single-storey cottages beyond the People's Drapery Warehouse (far left) has survived. One of the cottages, known as the Pale House, was used by Armadale's first Friendly Society to store their funeral hearse, which they hired out, requiring only that clients supply their own driver and horse.

This early view, captioned Station Road on the original postcard, actually shows South Street, since the latter extended as far as Bathville Cross. Off to the right, at 'bowling green corner', is the entrance both to James Wood public park and to the bowling green itself. The park was the gift of businessman James Wood, whose local assets alone included (in addition to his Armadale residence, Bathville House), 52 properties, an oil store, brickworks, wagon works and a locomotive shed. The bowling green, which was laid out some 35 years before the public park, had previously been the site of the Monkland Iron (or, as it was better known, Buttries) Company, which manufactured bricks. Although many of the properties seen here on South Street, including the row of single-storey cottages alongside the entrance to the public park, have survived, the taller two-storey tenement beyond the cottages has been demolished and replaced by newer housing.

In the sixteenth century the ancient Barony of Ogilface, which included Bridge Castle, came into the possession of William Livingstone, Earl of Linlithgow. At that time the castle (also referred to as the Fortalice of Little Brighouse) consisted of no more than a four-storey L-shaped tower occupying an elevated position above the Barbauchlaw Burn, three miles north of Armadale. In the seventeenth century a four-storey extension was built, with a further extension to the north-west being added in more recent times. In the 1870s – when the castle was in a ruinous condition and lacking a roof – it was renovated and extensively altered internally in the Victorian style by the owner James Maitland Wardrop. After renovation there were 33 rooms, the most notable being the banqueting hall with its vaulted ceiling. Around the turn of the twentieth century the castle was the home of Captain Thomas Hope. After it was sold by the Hope family, it was said to have been bought by Robert Young who, it is thought, was either the son or grandson of James 'Paraffin' Young of shale-oil fame. In 1940 it was acquired by a Robert Speir and, in the early 1960s, inherited by his daughter and her husband, Wing Commander D. Mackenzie. At that time it was thought to be one of the longest continuously inhabited houses in Scotland. By the early 1970s it had been further converted and, for a period, operated as the Castle Hotel. After the demise of the hotel, the building was converted internally in the mid-1980s and turned into luxury apartments.

The former Tippethill Fever Hospital, described at its opening as being 'magnificently-appointed', was built on high ground almost equidistant between Armadale and Whitburn. Opened in November 1901, it was initially run by a Joint Hospital Board made up of representatives from Bathgate, Whitburn and Armadale. Around 1902, following a widespread outbreak of smallpox, a smallpox pavilion was added. After the eradication of this disease, the wooden-framed pavilion was reused as a sanatorium for patients in the first stages of consumption. Although the hospital was extended on several occasions, by the early 1950s changing attitudes to health care led to a debate about its future role. Eventually, it was decided that the hospital should be closed and replaced with a new £2.3 million community hospital and sensory resource unit, to be built on the same site. On 28 March 2001 the new community hospital, Tippethill House, was opened by Susan Deacon, the Scottish Health Minister.

James Wood's interest in providing a public park was first expressed in 1891 when, in a letter addressed to the Armadale Commissioners, he noted that 'during my residence here I have observed the want the town of Armadale and neighbourhood has of a field of recreation and a hall for lectures, concerts and other public entertainment'. To address his first concern, he gifted a field to the west of the bowling green and equipped it with, in addition to the bandstand seen here near the entrance to the park, a drinking fountain, maypole and swings. The official opening took place on 26 June 1902, when Provost Adam Wilson presented their benefactor with an illuminated copy of his speech. Although no longer standing, during its lifetime the bandstand was one of the park's most popular facilities. In particular it attracted large numbers of spectators when bands such as the Armadale Silver Band used it for their popular summer Sunday afternoon and weekday evening concerts.

The desire for a local bowling green was expressed in the mid-1800s when the so-called 'shopkeeping' classes lost interest in the previously more popular sport of cricket. This new interest led, in 1867, to the formation of Armadale Bowling Club on ground to the rear of Monklands Cottage on South Street, which was acquired from the Laird of Barbauchlaw. Although the construction of the bowling green was easily funded by members' subscriptions and concerts, its maintenance proved slightly more problematic because of the various mine workings that ran underneath it. By 1914, when this photograph was taken, members could reflect with some satisfaction that their endeavours some eight years previously had also equipped the club with a splendid pavilion, seen here to the rear of the green. There would also no doubt have been further satisfaction from the knowledge that, even at this early stage in its lifetime, the club had already won the coveted County Bowling silver bowl on no fewer than six occasions.

In this view of Station Road, taken around 1905 and looking back towards Armadale Cross, the primitive and hazardous nature of the road from Armadale Cross to the railway station is only too apparent. The rutted road surfaces often proved especially tricky for the several carters who came into Bathville each day with goods such as fresh and 'soor' milk, butchermeat and fish. Inevitably there were many accidents, including one memorable occasion when the Armadale Co-operative Society's bread salesman's horse ended up with its head through the window of Lockhart Vidler's barber's shop window at Bathville Cross. Equally well remembered by older citizens is fruit and vegetable salesman Tam Thomson. Seemingly, Tam's horse, without prompting, would come to a halt at each of Tam's regular stops, which (probably not by chance!) often coincided with some of Tam's favourite watering holes.

Bathville (or Harestanes as it was known until 1797) was formerly Armadale's industrial district and was once only too recognisable by the heavy black smoke that constantly poured from around 44 tall chimneys. In the main, the miners employed locally were housed in single-storey terraced housing, known as 'rows', similar to that in Hardhill Terrace, seen here on the right of the photograph. Built by their employers, the houses were of the 'room and kitchen' type, and lacked many of the basic amenities which we take for granted today. Before 1883, for example, when both gas lighting and piped water supplies were introduced into the district, all water required for drinking or washing had to be carried in buckets from outside wells into the houses. Hot water for washing clothes (there were no wash-houses) and for baths (an essential in all mining families) had to be obtained by boiling big pots of water on the coal-fired iron ranges, which were also used for cooking.

In 1861 a station (which merely consisted of a small waiting room and booking office) was opened to the south of Armadale, at Cappers, on the former Monkland Railway's Bathgate and Coatbridge line. The station (seen here around 1907) was some distance from the centre of Armadale, and located on higher ground (at the 'tap o' the toun'). Despite its inconvenient situation, the regular daily services to Glasgow and Edinburgh meant that the line was fairly well used. However, passenger services were withdrawn in 1956, followed by freight traffic in 1961.

On Saturday, 6 May 1961 the Class N15 0-6-2 tank engine shown here pulled into Armadale Station carrying railway enthusiasts on a special Bathgate & District Railtour. Organised by the Branch Line Society, the railtour commenced in Glasgow, at Maryhill Central, and finished at Glasgow's Queen Street high level station. During its journey the train passed over several local lines, all of which, sadly, had by then been closed. At Sunnyside Junction in Coatbridge, for example, the train joined the former Airdrie to Bathgate line, calling briefly at, among others, Westcraigs and Armadale stations. From Armadale, the train proceeded to Bathgate and, following a short diversion to Avonbridge, it joined the former Wilsontown, Morningside and Coltness line, passing through Whitburn, Bents and Fauldhouse. By 1961 the track on the section of line between Fauldhouse and Castlehill Junction had already been lifted, so the railtour was then obliged to retrace its steps for part of the journey back to Glasgow.

Small shunting locomotives, or 'puggies' as they were more familiarly known, were commonly used by collieries for the transportation of coal and other waste products from the pits to the various local works. The puggie seen here was one of three belonging to United Collieries Limited, whose head office was in Glasgow but who maintained an office and workshops at their Bathville Works in Armadale. Although built by Martyn Brothers at their Chapelside Works in Airdrie, this particular puggie was based on a Dick & Stevenson design, that company having been taken over by Martyn Brothers around 1900. For much of its life the puggie operated between Westrigg Colliery and the fireclay works at Bathville, before being retired from service and scrapped in 1938. In one publication a former miner recalls that it was quite common to see James Wood, the chairman of United Collieries Limited, standing on the footplate of one of these puggies travelling to his Westrigg Pit.

Traditionally the waste products from the coal and shale-oil pits were used for the manufacture of bricks, both for the construction industry and for fire bricks used to line the walls of foundries. One of the early local brickworks was owned by John Watson, a Glasgow wholesale coal merchant and brick manufacturer, who acquired the Bathville estate in 1859. Shortly afterwards Watson died and the business was taken over by his sons William, Thomas and David. During its lifetime, the company built Quality Row (so called because it provided accommodation for foremen) and Bathville Row, which housed ordinary miners and their families. Bathville Row, which was the larger of the two, incorporated a well-stocked provisions store and a 'works' school. Despite its early success, the company was declared bankrupt in 1872 and was eventually acquired by James Wood.

In 1873, having expanded his business empire with the acquisition of land at Armadale, James Wood bought the Bathville estate, which then included Bathville House. The house, situated approximately half a mile to the east of Bathville Cross, was rebuilt by Wood and became his principal residence. He stayed there until 1902, when he moved to Torphichen. Initially, he retained the house and six acres of ground, but in 1905 he sold it to Alex McAra, a local grocer and proprietor of the Bathville Store and Inn. The house was later acquired by William Condie, a local auctioneer. In the early hours of Sunday, 3 February 1935, it was gutted by fire. Despite the alarm being raised immediately by a workman at a local brickworks, it proved impossible to save the building or its contents, and so the fire was left to burn itself out. The total damage was estimated at £5,000 and Bathville House was never rebuilt.

E. MARR, ARMADALE.　　　　　WOODLANDS, ARMADALE.

Unlike its near neighbour, Bathville House, Woodlands House has survived and is now divided into flats. It dates from around 1893 and was built for local coal merchant John King, whose company was later acquired by United Collieries Limited. In 1920 it was the home of the Rev. John Drew, minister of Armadale Parish Church. From the late 1930s until 1948 Woodlands House was the residence of Mr and Mrs James Watt. Watt, who was an associate of James Wood, was one of the founders of the Atlas Steel Company. His son, George Harvie Watt, served as Sir Winston Churchill's private secretary during the Second World War. After 1948 the house passed into the hands of the National Coal Board and from then until at least 1973 it was occupied by Coal Board officials.

This view of East Main Street was taken around 1918, looking east from the Cross. The two-storey building on the far left housed Elizabeth Kerr's People's Drapery Warehouse. The whitewashed gable end at the corner of North Street is the old Star Inn (later the Star Hotel), built in 1861 for a Mrs Ann Young, who in 1866 was threatened with legal action by the recently elected Armadale Commissioners should she fail to remove the 'pigsty, dungstead and privy' associated with her property. The Star Hotel is no longer there, but the taller two-storey building further down East Main Street is still standing. For most of the 1900s the ground floor of these premises was occupied by Giocondo Ugolini's popular café and fish restaurant. On the right of the photograph, at the corner of East Main Street and South Street, is Jacob Stirling & Co.'s licensed grocer's and tea merchant's business, which they owned from 1900 until around 1920. Further east, on the site of Wood Terrace, are the Russell Row miners' cottages.

On 6 October 1920, following the passing of the Housing (Scotland) Act 1919 (more commonly known as the Addison Act), Provost James Greig cut the first sod for the first council housing estate to be built in Armadale. The houses, including those seen here in Barbauchlaw Avenue, each had a living room, kitchen and bathroom, and one, two or three bedrooms. They were built to replace the single-storey miners' cottages known as Russell Row or, more familiarly the 'Raw', which had been built in the mid-1800s by Messrs Russell & Son, and were purchased by Armadale council from the Barbauchlaw estate around 1920. They were of the room-and-kitchen type, with outside toilets and wash-houses, and communal drying areas.

In June 1911 the Armadale Children's Day was expanded to include a special Coronation Festival, to celebrate the coronation of George V and Queen Mary. Dressed in their 'Sunday best', some of the children who participated in the parade are seen here on West Main Street, passing by Alex Hutton & Son's ironmongery shop and William Duncan's tailor's and clothier's shop. Although it had become standard during the annual Children's Gala Day to have flags, bunting, decorated floats and floral arches, a special addition for this coronation year only was the crowning of a Gala Queen. This was reintroduced in 1925 and it became a regular feature thereafter. Another addition to the 1911 Gala Day was the selling of 'temperance' refreshments from a tent in the James Wood Public Park, staffed by the local branch of the British Women's Temperance Society. This appears to have been allowed on condition that the 'temperance' refreshments did not include lemonade, as permission to sell this had already been given to a widow.

For most of the twentieth century, the ground floor premises of 25–27 West Main Street were occupied by J. M. Dickson's chemist's shop. As well as the usual range of medicines, a fairly large portion of what was, in effect, two shops, was set aside for the sale of cameras and other photographic equipment and film processing. When the pharmacy closed in the latter half of the twentieth century, Edinburgh businessman Victor Alongi reopened the premises as a fish and chip shop-cum-café and a restaurant. Alongi in turn sold the business to fellow Italians Nicandro and Concetta Coia, who continued to operate it as a fish and chip shop, using the former restaurant as a café in which they served their popular fish teas. Today, the fish and chip shop is owned by Piero Coia, Nicandro and Concetta's son.

For much of the seven years after his disastrous defeat at the Battle of Falkirk in 1298, William Wallace was a fugitive, forced into hiding to evade capture and likely execution. It is claimed that at times he sought refuge among the rocky wooded gorges of the River Avon, and local legend has it that one of his reputed hideouts was a naturally occurring sandstone archway, now known as Wallace's Cave. The existence of this 'cave' is described in the *New Statistical Account* of 1843 as being 'behind the mansion-house of Craw-hill, on the banks of the river Avon'. Today a modern footbridge known (perhaps not surprisingly) as Wallace Bridge, crosses the river at this point. This photograph shows Wallace's Lave, 'lave' being a term used by miners for the process of emptying out water, as well as for an old method of draining pits, suggesting perhaps that this is where Wallace came to drink. This, however, is only one of several local locations associated with Wallace, others being Wallace's Bed or Cradle, and Wallace's Stone.

From the sixteenth century the Bedlormie estate at Blackridge had been owned by the Livingstone family. In 1873 it was sold to Robert Young, a Glasgow iron and coal merchant, who within two years of his purchase replaced the existing Bedlormie House with the present house seen here. Originally built as a hunting lodge, it was later extended when it was acquired by James Wood. In 1902 Bedlormie House was one of many local properties acquired by the newly formed United Collieries Limited. Over the years the various owners of the house (known locally as the 'Big Hoose') involved themselves in the life of the village – at one time even allowing villagers to freely wander round the grounds. Among these past owners was Alexander Russell Ballantine, who served as one of the Public Hall trustees, and William Wilson, who was a member of the Torphichen Parish Council. Today, the house is divided into flats.

In this view, taken around 1911 from the top of the village looking east, some of the original single-storey cottages can be seen lining the north side of Main Street. These include Quarry Cottages, erected in 1897 by the Bowden Lime Company for their employees. Businesses operating here over the years include Wattie Neilson's cycle shop, where reputedly everything 'from a needle to an anchor' could be bought. Further along Main Street are the old police station and (in Cheyne's Buildings) the Auld Hoose Inn. While many of the properties on the north side of the street have survived, those on the right of the picture have all been demolished and this area is now the site of Blackridge Public Park. The demolished properties include Ashgrove Cottage, the premises of Mitchell Brothers hearse and horse-brake hiring business, a thatched cottage which was the first premises of the Blackridge branch of the West Benhar Co-operative Society, Robertson's Buildings, Quarry Buildings, and a property known locally as Babylon.

One of the longest-established businesses in Blackridge was the Mafeking Bakery, so called because it was opened for business just as the news of the Relief of Mafeking reached the village. The bakery was set up by John Brown, a Whitburn man, who had transferred the business to Blackridge. His premises stood on Main Street, opposite School Brae, on the site of the old toll house, and included a bakehouse, shop and house. Initially, the bread, biscuits and pastries prepared in the bakehouse were delivered around the district using the horse-drawn mobile shop shown here, but by the 1950s – and with the business now run by John's son Frank – all deliveries were made by a motorised van. In 1980 the bakehouse was sold to Dalziel of Airdrie. However, Frank's daughter Margaret and her husband John retained the shop, from which they sold and repaired televisions, in addition to selling groceries. Their shop was finally closed in late 2004, and also around this time the bakehouse collapsed.

Blackridge Public School on School Brae (seen here around 1907) was pre-dated by an earlier school erected in 1805 on Clattering Mill Road (near the present Louburn flats). In November 1876 this new and much larger school was opened on School Brae. Since 1895 the school has been extended on several occasions, notably at the turn of the twentieth century, when an influx of mining families created severe overcrowding – on one occasion, an infants' class capable of accommodating 70 pupils was required to accommodate 86. Further extensions to the school followed in 1911 and 1927, so that by 1931 the 641 pupils on the school roll were accommodated in three separate buildings containing a total of seventeen classrooms. In 1967, when a comprehensive education system was introduced, secondary pupils transferred to Armadale Academy, leaving the school to function solely as a primary school.

The annual Blackridge, Westrigg and Westcraigs Children's Gala Day was, from its inception around 1908, traditionally held on the last Saturday in June. In this early view, the parade (headed by pipers) is seen heading west along Main Street, passing the police station and Quarry Cottages. The parade usually started from the school and turnout was generally excellent. Children, complete with their 'tinny' around their neck, and some bearing banners and flags, would march to the local park. Once there, they would compete in races, five-a-side football games and tug-o'-war competitions. For a period, the Blackridge school tug-o'-war team was virtually unbeatable, at one time winning the county tug-o'-war championships for five consecutive years. Another popular children's event was the annual Sunday School trip. These would generally commence at Westcraigs Station, bound for places as far afield as Saltcoats or Ayr.

In this 1948 photograph, a contractor's lorry is seen crammed with children participating in the annual Blackridge Gala Day. Behind this is the Auld Hoose Inn, which stood on Main Street, at the foot of School Brae. An old-fashioned pub with sawdust-covered floors, it consisted of a main bar (generally a male preserve) and a smaller, separate 'jug' bar, or lounge. The latter tended to be used for quiet games of dominoes, and by the ladies. Over its lifetime the inn had a few names. Before 1911 it seems to have been called the Village Inn. It was also known locally as the 'Top' or 'Tap' Pub – to distinguish it from the Westcraigs Inn, or 'Bottom Shop'. In its final years, there was a further change of name to Broxi's – a reflection on the local support for a well-known Glasgow football team. The inn was badly damaged by fire in 2004 and was subsequently demolished.

In this early view of Blackridge Main Street, taken looking east, the stone-built cottage seen on the left comprised a grocery and a private house, known as Burnview Cottage. Over the years this grocery shop was run by, among others, Robert Murray, Calum Nimmo, Matt Skillen and Jack Skinner. Further along Main Street, at the top of Doctor's Brae, is Craig or 'Middle' Terrace. This was built in 1893 by James Nimmo & Sons for their employees. On the right of the photograph, nearest camera, is Billy Galbraith's wooden-hutted cobbler's shop and, alongside it, Woodside Terrace – now the site of Charles Tease's garage. Not shown, but also in this area, on ground off to the left, stands Manderwick. It was in this property, around 1893, that Isabella Storrie had her post office-cum-grocery shop. In the 1950s, under the ownership of Chrissie Souter, the business functioned as a post office-cum-newsagent's, but around 1986 the location of the post office was moved across the road to its present site in McFatter's Building.

In this 1906 photograph of Blackridge Main Street, taken looking west, the building on the far left was at one time a drapery, run in the 1960s by Cathy Davidson. The building next to this currently houses Andrew Sherlock's catering business. Previous to this it was William Liddell's butcher's shop, where at one time customers had to negotiate their way past hanging carcasses of slaughtered animals in order to reach the counter. Earlier still, these premises were occupied by the Dividend Stores and Walker's grocery. Just beyond the trees on the right are the single-storey cottages around Jardine Place. Here is located the Blackridge Masonic Lodge No. 1145. The lodge was established in 1915, but until around 1955 meetings were held in the Public Hall. It was in that year that the lodge purchased property in Jardine Place (which had formerly been Esau Edward's billiard parlour and ice cream shop). In 1978 it further expanded by purchasing an adjacent shop (formerly a newsagent's) and houses.

This late 1920s view shows the 'clattering' bridge and Barbauchlaw Burn. The burn was a favourite haunt of local children and this particular point was extremely popular for fishing for 'silver backed' and 'big beardie' minnons (minnows). Further up the burn were the areas known as the 'dook' and the 'big dook', where generations of Armadale children learned to swim. Also irresistible to children were the ruins of the old Clattering Mill, which had been in operation until the late 1800s and which was accessed via the footbridge – hence its name. On the left, among the trees, is the original Blackridge School. Despite its obvious deficiencies, both in respect of size and the condition of the building, nothing was done to improve it, with the result that, when responsibility was transferred to the newly elected Parish of Torphichen School Board, the school was described as being in a 'wretched' state. Later, when the new school was built at the top of School Brae, the old school was converted for use as a dwelling house, before finally being demolished. Also in this photograph, beyond the clattering bridge, can be seen Burnside Terrace and, to its right, Blackridge Public Hall.

Because of the tendency of Barbauchlaw Burn to overflow its banks and, temporarily at least, turn Burnside Terrace drying greens into a lake, locals often jokingly referred to the Terrace as Burnside Terrace by the Sea. During these times of flooding the outside toilets, inevitably, also became inaccessible. Burnside Terrace was the last of three terraces to be built by coal masters James Nimmo & Sons for their miners and families. Built in 1898, it was also known as 'bottom' Terrace, having been preceded by Craig (or 'middle') Terrace and Upper Craig (or 'top') Terrace. In the 1960s these three terraces (all of which can be seen here) were replaced with new council housing. Today Drummond Place stands on the site of Craig and Upper Craig Terraces, and the Louburn flats occupy the site of Burnside Terrace.

In this early view of Main Street, Blackridge, taken looking west, the buildings on the right are Blackridge Parish Church manse (now a private house called Mansefield) and the church. Before the erection of this church, adherents attended Armadale West Church, but in 1899, and despite concerns that there were already too many churches in the village, it was agreed to form a 'daughter' church in Blackridge. Although some of the cost was borne by the congregation, most of it (including the cost of the manse) came from Lady Baillie. Designed by Lothian-born architect James Graham Fairley, it was formally opened in October 1901. To the west of the church is Unity, a grey sandstone building which was built in 1902 and which, until about twenty years ago, was occupied by the West Benhar Co-operative Society's Blackridge Branch. On the opposite side of the street is Blackridge Public Hall, which was opened in 1910. Built on land gifted by James Wood, and paid for by public subscriptions and donations, it was, until its demolition in the late 1970s, a popular venue for meetings, dances, concerts and the much-loved picture shows (known locally as 'penny geggies').

This three-storey building is the original West Craig Inn, a former coaching inn built around 1795 to provide accommodation and stabling for travellers using the new turnpike or 'Great' road. As it was situated almost halfway between Edinburgh and Glasgow, it was – until the opening of the Glasgow & Edinburgh Railway – a popular stop for coaches travelling along the new road. Although trade declined after the opening of the railway, the inn still attracted visitors seeking overnight accommodation, and it is said that in Victorian times it was popular with honeymooning couples. When the inn was finally closed around 1843, the buildings were reused for farming. In October 1952, while in the ownership of Harry Johnston, most of the roof of Westcraigs Farm was destroyed in a blaze, causing considerable damage. In 1994 the farm was bought by the District Council and, with three-quarters of a million pounds' worth of funding from Rechar, a new community centre, library and museum was opened on the site. On 1 April 2000 the main farm building, which had been lying derelict, was restored in partnership with the Canmore Housing Association and opened as sheltered housing accommodation.

This late 1920s view of Main Street, Blackridge, taken looking east, shows the houses at MacLean Terrace, erected in 1922 by United Collieries Limited. In total fourteen houses were built, specifically for the company's managers, although for a period the two most westerly ones were bought, or leased, by Lothian & Peebles Joint Police Committee to provide accommodation for the village bobbies and for a charge room. In the main these houses have survived and, externally at least, are largely unchanged. To the east of MacLean Terrace, beyond the junction of Heights Road (on the left) and Westcraigs Road (on the right), at Westrigg, can be seen the newly erected houses forming Craig Inn Terrace. The taller two-storey property in the distance, beyond Craig Inn Terrace (on the site of the present Fleming Place) was known as Store block, presumably because the company store was located there, as well as homes for miners working in nearby Westrigg Colliery. This building has now been demolished.

For most of the twentieth century Agnes Gentleman's little wooden grocery shop stood on Westcraigs Road, at the entrance to Station Road. Handily placed for Westcraigs housewives and for the railway station, it sold a range of groceries, sweets and cigarettes. With the exception of the war years, when her sister helped in the shop, the business was run solely by Agnes. Following her retirement in the mid-1970s, the shop lay empty for a period, until it was ultimately condemned and taken down. The houses behind the shop on both sides of Westcraigs Road were built in the mid-1920s by United Collieries Limited.

In 1862 a railway line linking Glasgow and Edinburgh was completed. This was the second line to link these two cities and was built primarily for freight. A decade later (in February 1871) a passenger service was introduced on the line, with a stop at Westcraigs (to serve Harthill and Blackridge). The following year a stationmaster's house was built, and in the 1890s the station facilities were overhauled and a booking office, stationmaster's office, waiting rooms and toilet facilities were added. In addition, since most freight coming into Blackridge and Harthill came by rail, it was decided to equip the station with sidings, sheds, a crane and loading bays. Although the line was well used by local residents, passenger services ceased in January 1956. Over ten years later, in June 1967, the line was also closed to goods traffic. Thereafter the line was lifted and all the station buildings, with the exception of the stationmaster's house, were demolished. Today the site of the line forms part of a popular 14-mile walkway and cycle path, although there are currently plans to reopen the line.

Although Blackridge residents were eventually able to use the Glasgow–Edinburgh line for business and pleasure, it was primarily designed to serve the many collieries and other works which had sprung up in the West Lothian area throughout the 1700s and 1800s. Of the several local collieries, the Westrigg colliery, seen here to the east of the station, was one of the most important to the local economy. Although the Westrigg coal seam was first worked by the Westrigg Coke Company, this was only in a small way, and it was not until James Wood took over the colliery in 1888 that mining operations were significantly expanded. In his tenure, and later under the United Collieries Limited, new shafts were sunk and a power station, washing plant and other facilities were introduced. After the closure of the colliery in 1955, the huge coal bing remained – this can be seen in the distance, behind the stationmaster's house – although this has now gone. Nowadays some people feel that it is important that a bing should be preserved as a monument to the industry.

These cottages were erected at Northrigg in the 1860s by United Collieries Limited to house miners working in their nearby colliery. A traditional miners' 'row', the cottages consisted of 10 single-ends and 24 room-and-kitchen houses. Typically, the houses had brick floors and lacked damp-proof courses and ventilation. They were equipped with basic 'middens', and there were no wash-houses, coal cellars or gardens. Other than a small company store, the nearest amenities, such as shops, schools, churches and public houses, were in nearby Blackridge. The hardships these families faced – subject as they were to such things as the fluctuating fortunes of the colliery and coal strikes – are amply demonstrated in the old school log books. During one coal strike, it is recorded that every child was given a syrup roll and a dip of warm milk for their breakfast, and one or two cups of cocoa and another syrup roll for their dinner – probably the total of their meals for the day.